UFOS AND ALIENS

Sarah Fleming

Editorial consultants: Cliff Moon,
Lorraine Petersen and Frances Ridley

RISING ★ STARS

nasen Helping Everyone Achieve

nasen
NASEN House, 4/5 Amber Business Village, Amber Close, Amington, Tamworth, Staffordshire B77 4RP

Rising Stars UK Ltd.
22 Grafton Street, London W1S 4EX
www.risingstars-uk.com

Every effort has been made to trace copyright holders and obtain their permission for use of copyright material. The publisher will gladly receive information enabling them to rectify any error or omission in subsequent editions. All facts are correct at time of going to press.

Published 2007

Cover design: Button plc
Cover images: Alamy
Text design and typesetting: Andy Wilson
Publisher: Gill Budgell
Project management and editorial: Lesley Densham
Editing: Deborah Kespert
Editorial consultants: Cliff Moon, Lorraine Petersen and Frances Ridley
Illustrations: Patrick Boyer: pages 20–21, 30–31, 38–41
Oxford Illustrators and Designers: pages 5, 14, 15, 17, 18, 25, 26, 28
Paul McCaffrey: pages 4, 7, 18, 19, 22–23, 43
Photos: AKG-Images: pages 10 (Columbia Pictures/Album/AKG), 13 (top – 20th Century Fox/Vollmer, Jurge; bottom – Lucasfilm/20th Century Fox/ALB)
Alamy: pages 5, 6, 8, 9, 11, 16, 24, 27, 43
Darryl Barker Productions: page 32
Corbis: pages 26, 33, 37
Fortean Picture Library: pages 6 (Stephen C. Pratt/Fortean Picture Library), 9 (Werner Burger/Fortean Picture Library), 36 (Andy Radford/Fortean Picture Library)
Getty Images: pages 12, 26, 28, 29, 36, 42
Kobal: pages 10, 13, 35

British Library Cataloguing in Publication Data.
A CIP record for this book is available from the British Library.

ISBN: 978-1-84680-190-7

Printed by Craft Print International Limited, Singapore

NEWCASTLE UPON TYNE CITY LIBRARIES	
C432376700	
Bertrams	14.07.07
J001.942	£6.00

Contents

What is a UFO?

A **UFO** is something you see flying in the sky. You don't know what it is.

What could it be?

A bird?   An aeroplane?   A balloon?   A spaceship?

What's that?

4

Often, UFOs turn out to be something you can explain.

Some clouds can look like UFOs.

But do some UFOs come from outer space?

Do some UFOs have **aliens** in them?

Near or far?

It's hard to tell how far away an object is in the sky. It could be a big object far away. Or it could be a small object that's nearer.

5

What do UFOs look like?

UFOs come in many shapes.
These are the shapes most people see.

Round flying saucers

Long, thin spaceships

Schoolboy Stephen Pratt photographed this fly-past of UFOs from his home in Conisbrough, South Yorkshire, UK, on 28th March, 1966.

At night, UFOs can just be strange lights.
Where might these lights come from?

A bright planet
  or a star?

An aeroplane?

A searchlight?

A spaceship?

What else could be UFOs?

If **UFOs** aren't **alien** spaceships, what are they?

As well as birds and aeroplanes,
UFOs could be ...

The Northern Lights

This is a strange, bright glow that sometimes appears in the sky.

Ball lightning

This kind of lightning hangs in the air for a few seconds.

Shooting stars

These are small, fiery balls of rock that burn up as they fall to Earth.

UFO study

The UK **government** did a four-year study about UFOs. They decided UFOs did NOT **exist**. The study said that every report about UFOs could be explained in other ways.

There is not enough **proof** to say that UFOs exist.

But some people still believe that UFOs are real.

9

Little green man

People have written about 'little green men' and 'grey' **aliens** for more than one hundred years. They have appeared in films and on TV.

'Mars Attacks!' alien

A 'grey' from 'Close Encounters of the Third Kind'

10

Before people went into space, they thought aliens might live on Mars. They believed aliens would look a lot like people.

An alien from 'Star Trek'

Why do aliens on TV look like people?

◎ It's cheaper this way.

◎ It's easier to do the make-up.

◎ It's how the writer wanted the alien to look.

Other aliens

Aliens don't need to look like humans. They don't even need heads or arms. They could be big or tiny. They could be bad or good.

This is the alien from 'Alien', the movie.

Predator from
the film
'Alien V Predator'

Baddie gremlins
from the film
'Gremlins 2'

Chewbacca with
Han Solo from
'Star Wars'

13

UFO history

The name **UFO** was first made up in 1952 but people have always seen strange things in the sky.

Here are some possible UFO sightings.

Ancient Greece, 329 BC

Did Alexander the Great see UFOs? He reported 'flashing shields' diving at his army.

America, 1492 AD

Did Christopher Columbus see UFOs on his way to America? He reported lights flashing in the sky. But they may have been a storm, in the distance.

15

Pilots on both sides in World War II reported seeing **UFOs**. They said they looked like 'balls of fire' following the aeroplanes. Pilots called them 'foo fighters'.

World War II, 1939–45

What were foo fighters?

No one knows what foo fighters were but here are some ideas.

- fiery balls of lightning
- secret enemy aeroplanes
- alien spaceships

16

New York, 1974

Beatles' pop star, John Lennon, saw a UFO above his flat. He said it was so close he could have thrown something at it.

Album art

On the cover of his album 'Walls and Bridges', John Lennon wrote:

On the 23rd August 1974 at 9 o'clock, I saw a UFO. JL

17

Taken by aliens

Some people say they have been kidnapped by **aliens**.

They are taken into **UFOs**.

Aliens do tests on them. Some people get skin burns.

Sorry dear, I think I'm a bit late.

Late! You've been missing for five days!

When they get back to their real life, they find a long time has gone by. They feel dizzy.

18

UFO Kidnap!

Betty and Barney Hill say they were kidnapped by aliens last week.

They say a UFO came out of the sky and chased their car. It hovered above them. Then they found themselves in a spaceship.

The Hills cannot remember exactly what happened in the spaceship but they were very frightened. They woke up back in their car

Our artist shows the Hills about to be beamed into the UFO.

19

Kidnapped! (Part one)

It was following me! Faster!

I pedalled as hard as I could, but the **UFO** was catching up. It was getting closer, lower, following me across the park.

'Zzzzwhoom!'

I looked back. A beam of light shot out from the UFO. My bike swayed and I crashed in a heap on the grass.

The UFO kept coming. My legs were trapped under the bike. I couldn't run.

20

It had been just another normal Saturday. I was on my way to Ben's house, cycling across the park.

I saw a flashing light in the sky first, but it got bigger and bigger. It became a round metal **disc** – a flying saucer.

Somehow I *knew* it was after me, and I started to ride for my life.

And here I was, trapped by my bike, with the light beam coming across the grass …

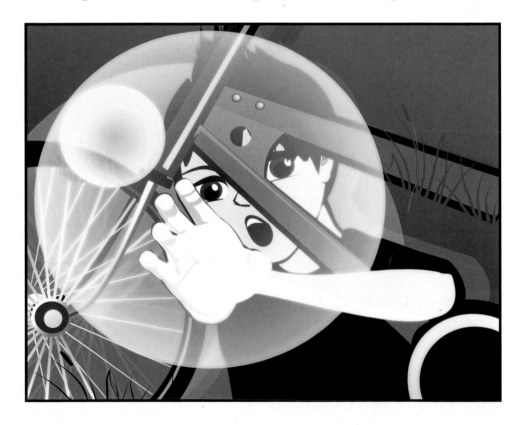

Continued on page 30

Rendlesham

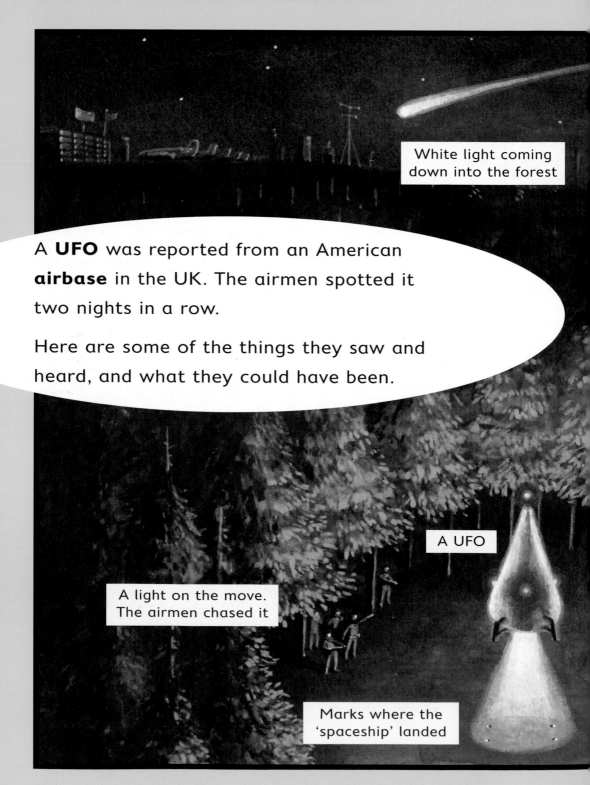

White light coming down into the forest

A **UFO** was reported from an American **airbase** in the UK. The airmen spotted it two nights in a row.

Here are some of the things they saw and heard, and what they could have been.

A UFO

A light on the move. The airmen chased it

Marks where the 'spaceship' landed

Case study

Date: 26th December, 1980

Strong lights

A flashing light

Something screaming

UK

Rendlesham Forest
Suffolk

23

Little Rissington

Two **RAF** pilots reported seeing **UFOs** in Gloucesershire in the UK. They had just flown out of the clouds.

Suddenly, they saw three white **discs** flying right in front of them.

Trained observers

People believe reports from **trained observers**, such as the police, **military** and pilots. These people are trained to report only what they see.

Case study

Date: October, 1952

At the same time, three 'blips' were seen on **radar** screens on the ground.

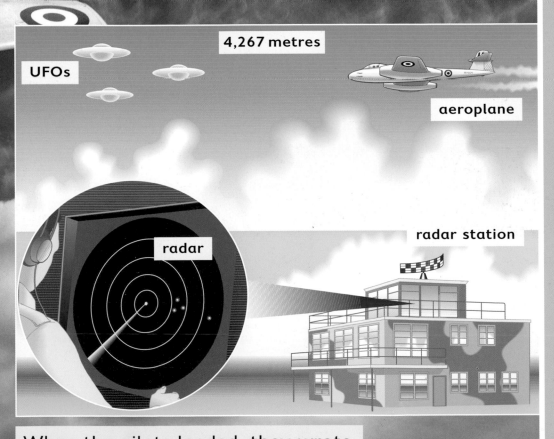

4,267 metres

UFOs

aeroplane

radar

radar station

When the pilots landed, they wrote about seeing the UFOs in their **log books**.

25

Roswell

In 1947, something crash-landed on a farm in the United States. **Military** men came to see it.

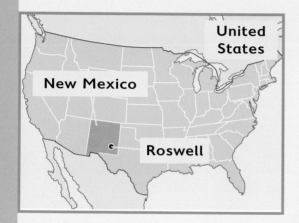

At first, the military said they had found parts of a **UFO**!

Later, they said it was a secret **weather balloon**.

Case study

Date: 2nd July, 1947

Roswell aliens?

A doctor said that he was made to cut open dead aliens from the crash.

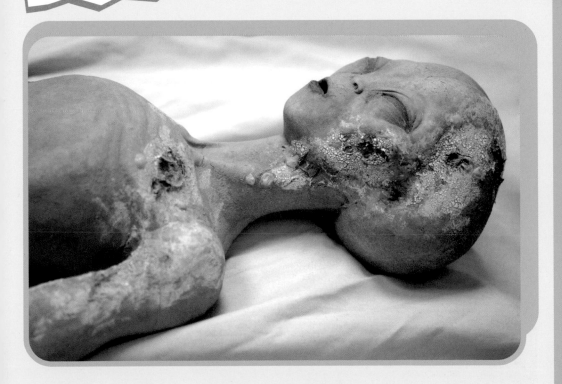

In 1995, someone 'found' a film of the Roswell alien being cut open on a table.

But the film was a **hoax**. Bits of dead sheep were used as the alien's insides.

27

Area 51

In the United States, there's a secret **airbase** called Area 51. You can't get in — it's 'off limits' to everyone.

The United States Air Force tests new aeroplanes here.

Some people think that **aliens** land at Area 51 to talk to the United States **military** and the **government**.

This spy plane was tested at
Area 51. Some people think aliens
helped to design it.

Kidnapped! (Part two)

I was in a white room, a big empty dome.

It hummed, and smelt of electricity.

I was inside the **UFO**. I wasn't afraid. Somehow I *knew* I would be OK.

A door slid open and an **alien** came out. It was small and grey, with big black eyes.

It didn't say anything, but I knew what to do. I followed it back through the door.

In the next room, there was a big bench.
I knew the alien wanted me to lie on it,
so I did.

The alien leant over me, and stared into my
eyes. It was reading my mind.

I could suddenly remember everything about
my life: being born, lying in a pram, a toy
I'd had when I was two, learning to ride
my bike …

Continued on page 38

31

Black triangles

Black triangle **UFOs** are as big as a football field and can fly slower and faster than any known plane.

Black triangles have been spotted all over the world.

March 30, 1990: Ans, Belgium

2,700 people saw a black triangle UFO. The Air Force sent F-16 planes to follow it. They tracked the UFO on **radar**, but it got away.

32

March 12, 1990: Moscow, Russia

People spent the night on their rooftops to watch groups of UFOs, including black triangles and flying saucers.

January 5, 2000: Illinois, USA

Five policemen, in different places, reported a black triangle UFO. The policemen all passed **lie detector tests**.

This silent spy plane looks like a black triangle UFO.

Close encounters

Researchers **classify UFO** reports.

One system classifies reports like this:

What was seen	How far away?	Type of report	Code
Lights in the night sky	More than 152 metres	Nocturnal Lights	NL
Strange objects in the distant daytime sky	More than 152 metres	Daylight discs	DD
Objects by eye and on **radar**	More than 152 metres	Radar/ Visual cases	RV

This is a DD report.

34

Steven Spielberg called this movie 'Close Encounters of the Third Kind'.

What was seen	How far away?	Type of report	Code
Strange objects in the sky	Closer than 152 metres	Close **Encounter** 1	CE1
Proof that a UFO was there e.g. landing marks	Closer than 152 metres	Close Encounter 2	CE2
Aliens	Closer than 152 metres	Close Encounter 3	CE3

Real or fake?

Here are some photos of **UFOs**.
Do you think they're real or fake?

1

Is this a real UFO above the trees or a fake?

2

What about this?
Is it real or a fake?

This photo was taken in 1966. It's too old to be faked on a computer. Is there a scratch on the photo?

Kidnapped! (Part three)

The **alien** took some little round things from under the bench.

It laid them on my head, my feet, my body and my hands.

The room hummed louder and the round things fizzed on my skin.

The humming stopped and the alien took off the round things. It put them on the bench.

It was time to go.

I wanted something to take with me, to prove I'd been there.

I got up from the bench and put out my hand to pick up one of the round things.

Arghh! It was freezing cold! My hand jerked back and I saw a mark on my palm.

The alien was watching me. If it could have smiled, I think it would have.

I followed it back through the door and everything just faded away...

Continued on the next page

39

Kidnapped! (Part three)

"Rob! Rob! Are you OK?"

I opened my eyes. Ben was bending over me. I was lying against a tree in the park. My bike lay beside me.

"What happened?" he said.

"Wha …?"

"Where have you been? Are you OK? You've been gone for hours."

He continued, "I called your house when you didn't come. Your mum said you'd left four hours ago! She wanted to call the police, but I said I'd check in the park first."

Four hours! It seemed like I'd only been in the **UFO** for ten minutes.

I looked at my hand. There was a red, round scar in the palm.

"Ouch!" said Ben "Was that your bike? Did you crash?"

I *knew* where I'd got that scar. But should I tell Ben? Would he believe me?

Is anything out there?

Do **aliens** exist? Are we alone?

There may be hundreds of millions of planets in the **universe**. Is there life on any of these planets?

If there is life, maybe it will send a **radio signal**. People are listening for signals from space. If we heard a signal, we would know there was life.

And maybe it would come and see us ...

It's a fact!

Fifty-seven per cent of Americans believe that **UFOs** visit us from outer space.

Quiz

1 In the daytime, what could you mistake for a UFO?

2 What are the two shapes of UFO most people see?

3 At night, what could you mistake for a UFO?

4 For how many years have people written about 'little green men'?

5 Can you name two famous people from history who have seen UFOs?

6 What were 'foo fighters' in World War II?

7 What is a CE3 report?

8 Can you name two types of trained observer?

9 What kind of 'aliens' crashed at Roswell?

10 What is the name of the secret airbase where the United States Air Force tests new aeroplanes?

Glossary of terms

airbase — A military airport.

alien — A living thing from another world.

classify — To put things in classes or groups.

disc — A round, flat object.

encounter — To meet someone unexpectedly.

exist — To have life, or be real.

government — The group of people in charge of a country.

hoax — A trick.

lie detector test — A scientific test which can tell if someone is lying or not.

log book — A book in which you write information about voyages.

military — Something to do with the armed forces – that's the army, navy or air force.

proof — A fact that shows that something is true.

radar — A system that uses radio waves to show the position of objects.

RAF — Stands for Royal Air Force. It is the UK's military force that uses aircraft.

radio signal — A series of radio waves that gives information.

trained observer — A person trained to watch things carefully.

UFO — Stands for Unidentified Flying Object.

universe — Everything that exists, including all of space and the stars and planets.

weather balloon — A balloon which carries instruments to send back information on the weather.

More resources

Books

**UFOs and Aliens,
The Unexplained series**
Colin Wilson
Published by Dorling Kindersley (ISBN: 075135984X)
An overview of the subject.

**UFOs: Alien abductions and close encounters,
Graphic Mysteries series**
Gary Jeffrey
Book House (ISBN: 1905087810)
This book tells the story of three UFO cases, including
Roswell, in cartoon form.

Websites

http://www.ufoevidence.org
This site has lots of reported UFO cases.

http://skepdic.com
This site does not believe in UFOs or aliens. It shows the other
side of the argument.

http://en.wikipedia.org/wiki/UFO
This online encyclopedia gives factual information about many
things, including UFOs and aliens.

Answers

1 Birds, balloons, clouds, spaceships, aeroplanes

2 Flying saucers and long, thin UFOs

3 Planets, shooting stars, lightning, other strange lights in the sky, searchlights shining on clouds

4 More than one hundred years

5 Alexander the Great, Christopher Columbus or John Lennon

6 Foo fighters was the name pilots gave to UFOs which followed their aeroplanes.

7 A CE3 report is a report about a Close Encounter 3.

8 People in the police, the military, or pilots

9 greys

10 Area 51

Index